A SEA CREATURE ATE MY TEACHER

Brian Moses lives in Sussex with his wife and has two daughters. He travels the country presenting his poems in schools and libraries.

Lucy Maddison is a slippery illustrator who lives in Streatham, London, with her partner Brian, daughters Sami and Katrina and an excitable hamster called Patch. None of her teachers were eaten by sea creatures, but one did get scared by a frog.

A SEA CREATURE ATE MY TEACHER

Seaside Poems chosen by
BRIAN MOSES

Illustrated by Lucy Maddison

MACMILLAN CHILDREN'S BOOKS

First published 2000 by Macmillan Children's Books

This edition published 2011 by Macmillan Children's Books
a division of Macmillan Publishers Limited
20 New Wharf Road, London N1 9RR
Basingstoke and Oxford
Associated companies throughout the world
www.panmacmillan.com

ISBN 978-1-4472-0019-2

3 5 7 9 8 6 4 2

A CIP catalogue record for this book is available from the British Library.

Printed and bound in the UK by CPI Group (UK), Croydon, CR0 4YY

'Plenty More Fish in the Sea' by Lindsay MacRae from *You Canny Shove Yer Granny off a
Bus!* Puffin 1996, by permission of The Agency Ltd on behalf of the author.

Contents

Rock and Roll Limpet

The limpet is a star

On the guitar

He plays

Jazz,

Blucs,

Country,

But he's

Best when

He sticks to

Rock.

John Coldwell

Seasick

'I don't feel welk,' whaled the squid, sole-fully.
'What's up?' asked the doctopus.
'I've got sore mussels and a tunny-hake,' she told him.

'Lie down and I'll egg salmon you,' mermaid the doctopus.
'Rays your voice,' said the squid. 'I'm a bit hard of
   herring.'
'Sorry! I didn't do it on porpoise,' replied the doctopus
   orc-wardly.

He helped her to oyster self onto his couch
And asked her to look up so he could sea urchin.
He soon flounder plaice that hurt.

'This'll make it eel,' he said, whiting a prescription.
'So I won't need to see the sturgeon?' she asked.
'Oh, no,' he told her. 'In a couple of dace you'll feel brill.'

'Cod bless you,' she said.
'That'll be sick squid,' replied the doctopus.

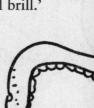

Nick Toczek

A Sea Creature Ate Our Teacher

Our teacher said that it's always good
To have an inquisitive mind,
Then he told us, 'Go check the rock pools,
Let's see what the tide's left behind.'

The muscles on his arms were bulging
As he pushed rocks out of the way.
'Identify what you see,' he called,
'Note it down in your book straightaway.'

It was just as he spoke that we smelt it –
A stench, like something rotten,
A wobbling mass of wet black skin
Like something time had forgotten.

In front of us snaking up from the pool
Was a hideous slime-soaked creature
With a huge black hole of a mouth
That vacuumed up our teacher.

I didn't actually see him go,
I was looking away at the time,
But I saw two legs sticking out
And trainers covered in slime.

But our teacher must have given this creature
Such chronic indigestion.
It found out soon that to try and digest him
Was simply out of the question.

It gave an almighty lunge of its neck
And spat our teacher out.
He was spread with the most revolting goo
And staggering about.

None of us moved to help him
As he wiped the gunge from his head.
We looked at each other and smirked,
'That'll teach *him* a lesson,' we said!

Brian Moses

Flying Fish

I've never seen a flying fish.
I've seen a load of birds.
Swallows, swifts and starlings
Ostriches and churds . . .
I'm always on the look out
For fishes flying by
A codfish or a haddock
A fishcake or a pie . . .
I'd really love to see one
I'd love to hear them sing
Pretty little feathers
Pretty little wings.
But:
I've never ever seen one
So, please remember me
If you see one in the bushes
Or nesting in a tree.

Peter Dixon

Water Music

There's an air of excitement deep under the waves;
There are sharks tuning up in the bottomless caves
For tonight there's a concert – they all take a part –
And each fish and each mollusc's rehearsing its art.
The upside-down-catfish conducts with his tail,
And the cymbals are clashed by a massive blue whale.
The clown fish, whose tenor is reedy and scratchy,
Is practising solos from 'I Pagliacci'.
The haddock are plucking their strings pizzicato,
A rather large prawn's trying out 'The Mikado'.
There's a dolphin duet on piano and scuba.
A conger eel's trapped in the coils of a tuba.
Three plaice sing 'Titanic' in voices that quiver.
A rumble of bass harmonise 'Ole Man River'.
The halibut practise their scales with a screech
And the tuna's big drum can be heard up the beach.
Every sea slug, crab, jellyfish, cod will appear
To perform – it's the concert event of the year.

Alison Chisholm

Coral Reef

I am a teeming city;
An underwater garden
Where fishes fly;
A lost forest
Of skeleton trees;
A home for starry anemones;
A hiding place for frightened fishes;
A skulking place for prowling predators;
An alien world
Whose unseen monsters
Watch with luminous eyes;
An ancient palace topped by
Improbable towers;
A mermaid's maze;
A living barrier built on
Uncountable small deaths;
An endlessly growing sculpture;
A brittle mystery;
A vanishing trick;
A dazzling wonder
More magical than all
Your earthbound dreams;
I am a priceless treasure;
A precious heirloom,

And I am yours

To love
Or to lose
As you choose.

Clare Bevan

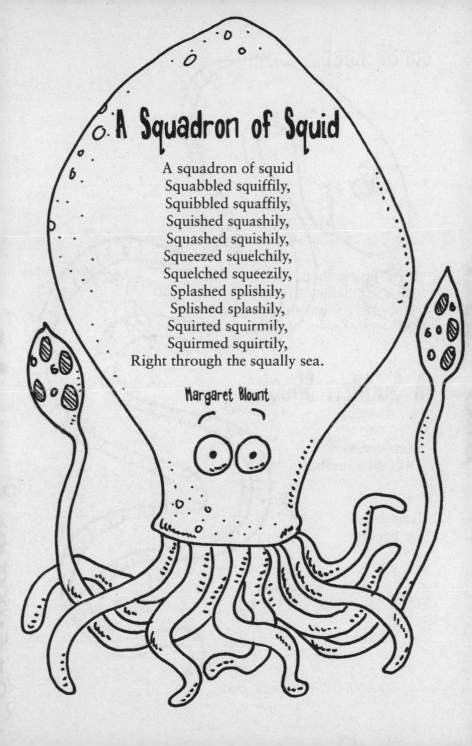

A Squadron of Squid

A squadron of squid
Squabbled squiffily,
Squibbled squaffily,
Squished squashily,
Squashed squishily,
Squeezed squelchily,
Squelched squeezily,
Splashed splishily,
Splished splashily,
Squirted squirmily,
Squirmed squirtily,
Right through the squally sea.

Margaret Blount

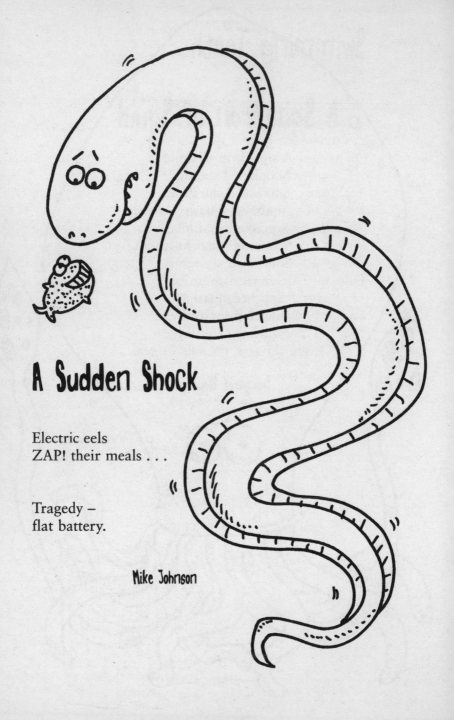

A Sudden Shock

Electric eels
ZAP! their meals . . .

Tragedy –
flat battery.

Mike Johnson

Swimming Teeth

I'm not a do-as-you're-told fish
A looked-at-in-a-bowl fish.
A stay-still-to-behold fish
An as-you-can-guess goldfish.

Where sea is blue, I make it red.
Where body bubbles, I slash, I shred.
Where eyes see light, I blur them dark.
Where skin shines bright, I expose a heart.

Humans call me shark.
But to my friends of the deep
I am known as SWIMMING TEETH
And one day I'd like to direct a movie.

John Agard

Puffer Fish

Those who think this little fish'll
Make a very tasty dish'll

Find as dinner starts to bristle
That they've bitten on a thistle!

Liz Brownlee

Mike the Mechanic

Mike the mechanic would like you to know
That he'll keep you moving if your batteries are low
He'll jump-start your motor while you're at the wheel
He's Mike the mechanic, the electrical eel.

He's trained to fix anything that might have gone wrong
He's always on call and he won't keep you long
Headlights or wipers, or pr'aps an oil seal
Nothing's too much for this electrical eel.

His garage is spotless, it's state of the art,
He'll never refuse you, he's got a kind heart
And when the sun's setting and day's getting dim
His workshop lights up as he plugs himself in.

Brian Grindall

A Doomed Love

It was the talk of seven oceans
The love affair that might have been
When the whale fell head over tail in love
With a submarine.

Roger Stevens

Plenty More Fish in the Sea

Do monkfish have habits
You'd better not mention
Do clownfish do tricks
Just to get some attention

Do tuna like music
Do parrotfish squawk
Do sole put on shoes
To go out for a walk

Can angelfish fly
Are skate cold and icy
Do turbots have engines
Is that why they're pricey

Do all fish have fingers
Do kingfish wear crowns
Is a haddock a hammock
Who's let himself down

Do perch sit like budgies
Do carp mope about
Is a snapper bad-tempered
Do blowfish all pout

Do grouper get lonely
In groups less than three
Don't they know
That there's plenty more fish in the sea?

Lindsay MacRae

Phantom of the Ocean

I'm a terrifying Portuguese man-o'-war
Phantom of the ocean, that's the score.
There's not a single creature no matter how vast
Doesn't rocket out of danger as I stream along past.

In and out of harbours among the fishing boats,
Water slapping round their hulls, drying nets and floats,
Faces peering down, disbelieving then aghast,
Screaming out the danger as I ripple past.
Hey, divers and swimmers, better look out.
There's a fearsome hydrozoan about.
With my blue-green translucent camouflage cap
I'm a spectral, blistering wrap-around trap.

Following the currents, swinging with the flow,
Patrolling sultry waters, always on the go,
Trailing tangled tentacles in ringlet strings
Like wire-wool unravelled, with an armoury of stings,
Topped by a glistening, pulsating jelly blob;
Catch a glimpse of me it'll make your head throb.

There's not a single creature, no matter how vast,
Doesn't rocket out of danger as I dangle past.
I'm a terrifying Portuguese man-o'-war
Phantom of the ocean, that's the score.

Penny Kent

The Rock-pool Rap

We're gonna put the rock-pool
Rap on the map
Do the cuttle-fish
Scuttle-fish
Rock-pool rap

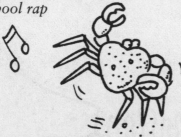

One foot forward
One foot back
Six-feet sideways
We like it like that.

We're gonna put the rock-pool
Rap on the map
Do the cuttle-fish
Scuttle-fish
Rock-pool rap

Papa's got a brand new crab!
(ooh)

Bless my sole
What's wrong with me
I'm shaking on the reef
At the bottom of the sea

The sea-squirt flirts
The stickleback's stickled
The rockling's rocking
And the sea-gherkin's pickled

20

We're gonna put the rock-pool
Rap on the map
Do the cuttle-fish
Scuttle-fish
Rock-pool rap

Prawn free
As free as the tide flows . . .

Suzie on the sea shore
Making a wish
The sandhopper's bopping
With the raspberry jellyfish

There's the Fiddler crab
Rocking up a storm
Everybody conga
With the shrimp and prawn

We're gonna put the rock-pool
Rap on the map
Do the cuttle-fish
Scuttle-fish
Rock-pool rap.

Roger Stevens

A School Trip

The Museum was great
and the youngsters had fun
inspecting the galleon
and admiring the guns.
The old Jolly Roger
once flew from the mast
but the galleon was wrecked
and the looting long past.
Skeletons (real ones)
sprawled, gruesome and pale,
then, seen in a skull,
the swift swish of a tail.
'Get out of those skulls,'
shrieked the teacher, 'you brats!'
and out of the sockets,
a school of young sprats
shot, curvetting, cavorting
in stingray formation.
'These school trips.' The teacher moaned.
'Pure irritation!
Next, the Titanic.'
She grumbled. 'First right.
The curator's a dogfish
and, watch out, he bites.'
Then they toured the Titanic,
(hard to resist)
and the dogfish ate several
who weren't ever missed.

Marian Swinger

Swordfish

I'd love to be a swordfish
said the mussel to the prawn
I hoped I'd be a swordfish
the day that I was born . . .

but God made me a mussel
and I'm stuck upon these rocks
and never ever travel
or wear nice shoes or socks.

Oh! I'd love to be a swordfish
a sea slug
or a squid
a crab
or dab or dolphin
a haddock or a cod.

But:
I was born to be a mussel
we are just who we are
my boyfriend thinks I'm lovely
my mum thinks I'm a star.

Peter Dixon

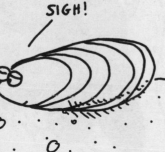

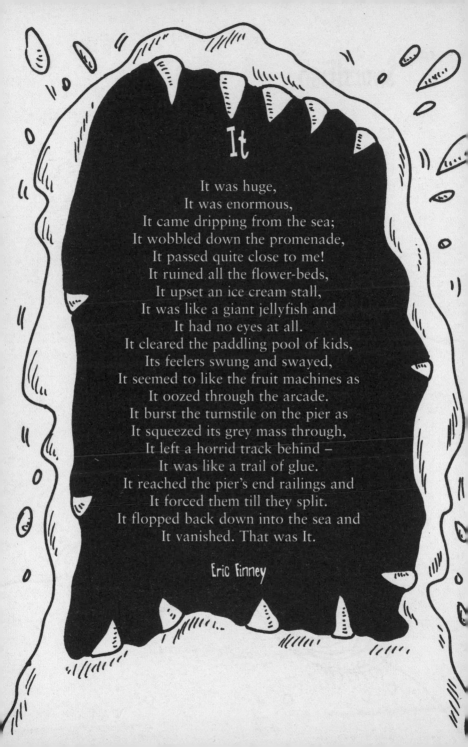

It

It was huge,
It was enormous,
It came dripping from the sea;
It wobbled down the promenade,
It passed quite close to me!
It ruined all the flower-beds,
It upset an ice cream stall,
It was like a giant jellyfish and
It had no eyes at all.
It cleared the paddling pool of kids,
Its feelers swung and swayed,
It seemed to like the fruit machines as
It oozed through the arcade.
It burst the turnstile on the pier as
It squeezed its grey mass through,
It left a horrid track behind –
It was like a trail of glue.
It reached the pier's end railings and
It forced them till they split.
It flopped back down into the sea and
It vanished. That was It.

Eric Finney

Neptune's Circus

Have you ever seen an octopus
Riding on a bike?
Have you ever seen a starfish
Balance on one spike?

Have you ever watched a great white shark
Cross the thin high wire?
Have you ever watched a dancing crab
Dive through hoops of fire?

Have you ever spied a giant squid
Juggling shells with ease?
Have you ever spied a humpback whale
Fly the high trapeze?

If not, but you would like to
See all these wondrous sights
Then come to Neptune's Circus
It starts at eight tonight.

Richard Caley

The Beast from the Deep Abyss

What lives in a watery grave?
The Beast from the deep abyss.
What's emerging from the waves?
The Beast from the deep abyss.
What is slippery? What is slimy?
What has scales so green and shiny?
What has seaweed cold and grimy?
Yes it is, yes it is . . .
The Beast from the deep abyss.

What has spikes around its head?
The Beast from the deep abyss.
What has suckers, round and red?
The Beast from the deep abyss.
What has fins that are ten feet long?
Twenty tentacles, coiled and strong?
What ate Moby Dick . . . and then King Kong?
Yes it is, yes it is . . .
The Beast from the deep abyss.

What has the teeth of a thousand sharks?
The Beast from the deep abyss.
What gave the electric eel its sparks?
The Beast from the deep abyss.
What sucks blood from living creatures?
Looks for prey upon the beaches?
What's so foul it eats up teachers?
Yes it is, yes it is . . .
The Beast from the deep,
The Beast from the deep,
The Beast from the deep abyss.

Paul Cookson

ARRGH!

HELP!

For the Love of a Mermaid

I'm an old sailor's skeleton
Lost deep down undersea.
I drowned so many years ago
The world's forgotten me.
My shipwreck is my only home
But after all these years
I've fallen for a mermaid,
I love everything of hers:

She's the dimples on a dolphin;
She's the freckles on a fish;
She's the blush on an octopus's cheek;
She's the manatee's elbows;
She's the nails of a whale;
She makes my bones go weak.

I'm an old sailor's skeleton
Lost deep down undersea.
She's a mermaid in a million,
Will she ever look at me?
My shipwreck is my only home
But after all these years
I'd like to take my mermaid
And make my shipwreck hers.

Celia Warren

29

Otto's Burger Bar

You've fished all morning from the pier
But not a single fish comes near
No flounder, dab or bass in sight
Not a nibble, not a bite
Where have they gone? Why do they go?
Just ask beneath the waves. They know!
Each sprat and fry; each Ma and Pa
They're all at Otto's Burger Bar

Far beneath the restless sea
Otto's is the place to be
Other joints find business slack
But Otto's bar is always packed
There's no live band or cabaret
Just Otto's dazzling display
For though his clientele has grown
Otto still runs things alone

Each guest he personally greets
Takes their coats and finds their seats
(Keeping predators away
From those they might regard as prey!)
He cooks the burgers, fries the chips
Cuts chicken nuggets, makes the dips
Brews the tea, pours fizzy drinks
Scrubs the floor and cleans the sinks

He waits at every single table
And some evenings, when he's able
Sings an old sea-song or two
Or plays a solo on kazoo
'How does he manage', you may ask
'To cope with each and every task?'
The answer's simple, but it's true
Eight hands can do much more than two!

Just watch his tentacles pulsate
One pours a drink, one scrubs a plate
One flips a burger, while another
Leads a sprat back to his mother
One peels spuds, one holds the door
One scrapes a mess up from the floor
And one puts the money in a great big jar
At Otto the Octopus's Burger Bar

Paul Bright

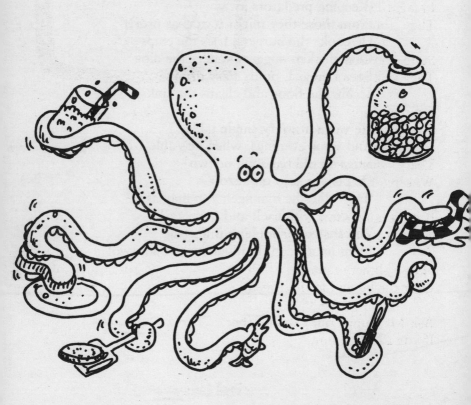

Fish TV

Staring at the school aquarium
Like a giant television.

When it's a Soap
The fish blow bubbles.

When it's educational
The fish swim in schools.

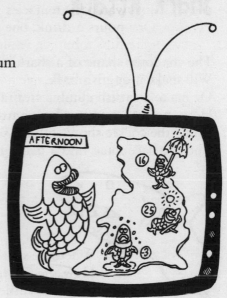

In a gardening show
They trim the weeds.

Sunday evenings
They sing about cod.

On the history channel
Fish swim through a tiny Greek pot.

There's one called Michael
Who reads the weather.

If it's a horror film
The big squid that somehow got in there

Slips a slithery tentacle
Over the lid and grabs a meal.

Ask Mr Guppy our class teacher
If you can find him.

David Harmer

Shark Attack

The shadowy shape of a shark
Will make a dogfish bark,
Or make a catfish climb a tree in fright.
How the hake and haddock hustle,
While the cockle shows his mussel,
And the dace must find a plaice that's out of sight.

When the shark is on the gobble,
How the jellyfish will wobble,
How the cuttle-fish will scuttle to its hole.
But the crayfish and the cod
Do the conger, which is odd,
And the ray can only pray to save its sole.

When the shark is being sharkish,
All the shellfish and the starfish
Hide the winkle in a twinkle from his jaws.
But the whiting will not wait
As the scallops try to skate,
And the sea-horse gallops off to hide indoors.

To avoid old sharky's gullet,
The mackerel and the mullet
Leave the roach and loach to flounder in the lurch.
But the tuna and the tunny
Can't see anyfin that's funny
When the flying-fish falls laughing off its perch.

When the shark has had his fill,
And he's feeling rather brill,
How the herring and the halibut will sigh.
How the turbot and the trout
And the shad will give a shout,
But the crab will dab a teardrop from its eye.

Now the shark has finished fishing,
And the wrasse and the bass are missing,
With the salmon and the sardine and the scat;
Let us find a fishy thought
For those clownfish that were caught:
I hope *you* won't be such a silly spratt!

How many fish can you count?

Mike Jubb

Sea Names

In the dark, weedy jungle
Of the deep, deep sea,
The strangest sea creatures
Wait for you and for me.

Alongside the sea-bream
Sea-anemones seem to slumber
With the grey sea-elephant
And the sea-cucumber.

There's also the sea-cow
And the odd sea-ear.
There's a sea-hare too
Near the end of the pier.

Who rides the sea-horse
Through the sea-lily seas?
Can you catch a sea-mouse
With a trap and salty cheese?

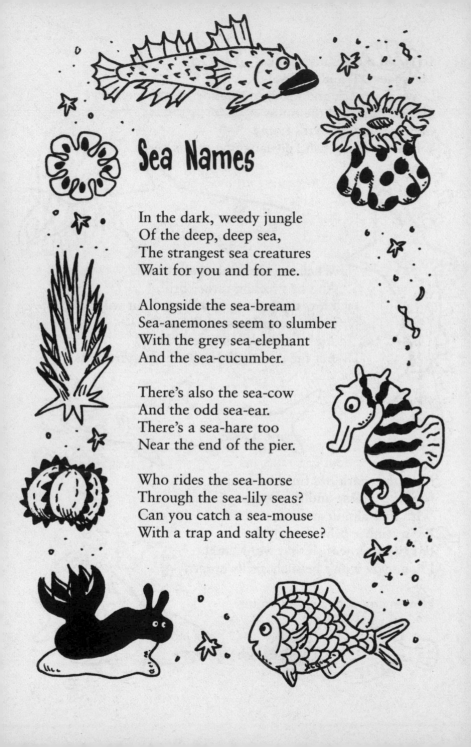

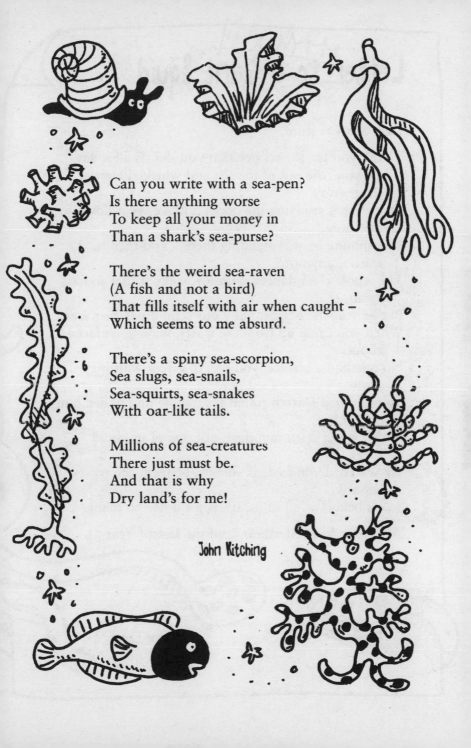

Can you write with a sea-pen?
Is there anything worse
To keep all your money in
Than a shark's sea-purse?

There's the weird sea-raven
(A fish and not a bird)
That fills itself with air when caught –
Which seems to me absurd.

There's a spiny sea-scorpion,
Sea slugs, sea-snails,
Sea-squirts, sea-snakes
With oar-like tails.

Millions of sea-creatures
There just must be.
And that is why
Dry land's for me!

John Kitching

Letter to a Giant Squid

Dear Sea Creature,

Thank you for the service that you did us all today,
When you rose out of the sea and whisked Darren
    clean away.
Our class is studying the ocean and we went down to
    the shore,
One minute he was standing there – and then he
    wasn't, anymore.
The whole class danced with joy, sorry if that sounds
    mean,
But he was the biggest bully our school has ever seen.
When you came up from the water, waving tentacles
    about,
No one had a chance, you see, to give a warning
    shout.
You grabbed Darren round his middle and pulled him
    off his feet,
We all stood open-mouthed, not one of us could
    speak.
We watched, amazed, as silently, beneath the waves
    he sank,
So on behalf of all of us, it's **you** I'd like to thank!

With love from Matthew (and the rest of Year 5).

Anne Logan

The Aquarium

The aquarium
was disappointing:

The dogfish
didn't bark,
the jellyfish
didn't wobble.

The sea mouse
didn't squeak,
the starfish
didn't shine.

The hermit crabs
were crabby,
the clams
clammed up,
and the plaice
stayed in one place.

But when the swordfish
attacked us,
and the sharks invited us
to be their lunch . . .

we rode away fast . . .
on a sea horse!

Brian Moses

Space Shuttlefish

When the moon shines bright on a starry night
And the ocean shimmers with pale moonlight,
Space Shuttlefish dreams of his destiny –
To swim in the Sea of Tranquillity.

The rocket science fish ask why
He wants to swim in a sea that's dry.
They tell him that it's lunacy.
He tells them it's a lunar sea.

Some call Space Shuttlefish a crank,
But he'll take with him a water tank.
He could be in the news quite soon –
The first sea creature on the moon.

Jane Clarke

THAT'S ONE SMALL STEP FOR MAN...

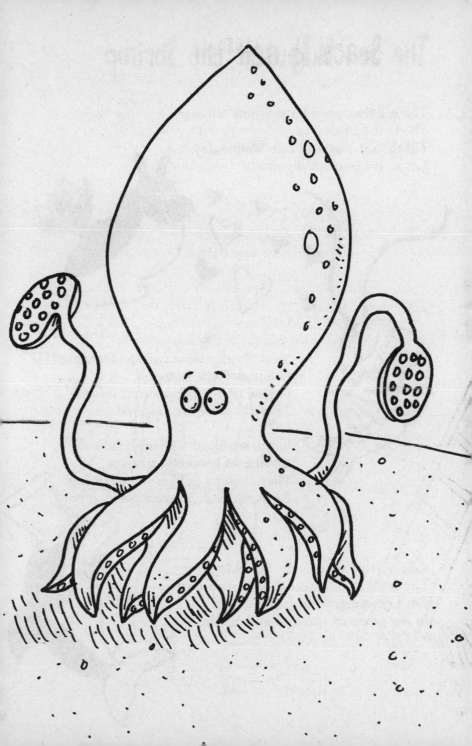

The Sea Slug and the Shrimp

The sea slug wooed a shy pink shrimp
The best part of a year,
Till the sea slug said one Wednesday,
Let us get hitched, my dear.

Miss Shrimp went two shades pinker.
O Samuel! she stuttered,
*I think that is the sweetest thing
That you have ever uttered.*

In the wreck of a Spanish galleon,
Among its sparkling treasure,
They found a golden wedding ring
Perfectly made to measure.

Sidney Dolphin was the Best Man,
The bridesmaids were the Jellyfish Girls,
Jim Lobster gave the bride away
In her gown of seaweed and pearls.

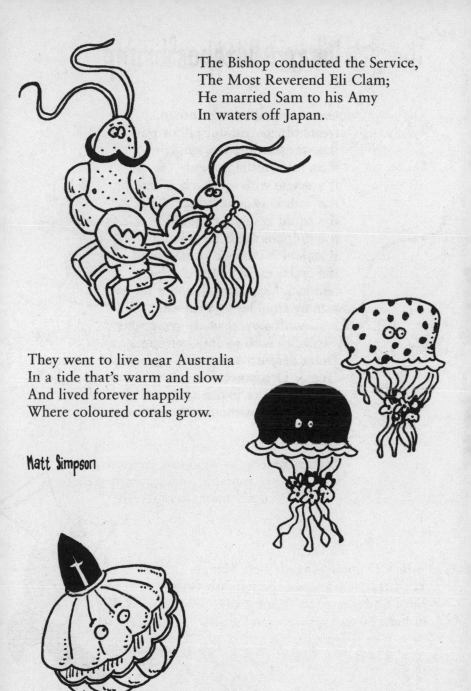

The Bishop conducted the Service,
The Most Reverend Eli Clam;
He married Sam to his Amy
In waters off Japan.

They went to live near Australia
In a tide that's warm and slow
And lived forever happily
Where coloured corals grow.

Matt Simpson

Doctor Octopus

Greatest healer in the ocean,
treats illness without pill or potion:
if a sturgeon needs a surgeon
if an eel is feeling queasy
if a whale with toothache's wailing
if a walrus is quite wheezy
if a squid is slightly squiffy
if a dolphin needs de-waxing
if a clam is jammed or damaged
if a crab's claws need relaxing;
haddock headache, flounder fin-rot,
tummy troubles of a turbot,
seals with several sickly symptoms,
barnacles with pimply bottoms . . .
Don't despair! Don't give up hope –
Doctor Octopus can cope:
greatest healer in the ocean,
treats illness without pill or potion.

Mike Johnson

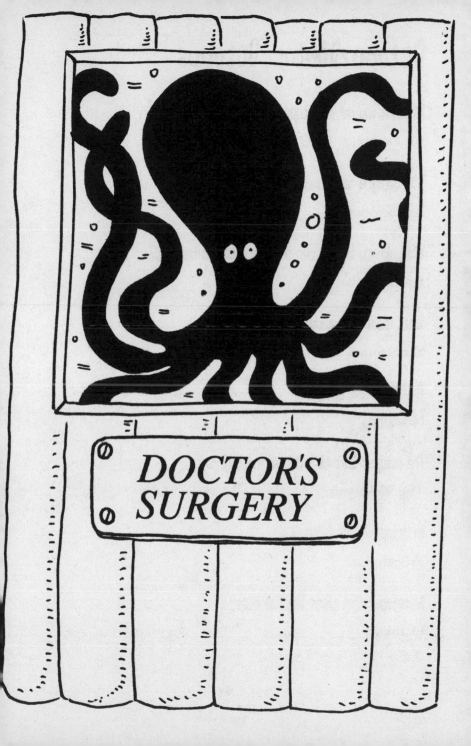

Octopuzzles

What do you call an octopus with ten legs?

An Octoplus . . . Octoplus Two to be exact.

What do you call a medical octopus?

A Doctopus.

What do you call an alien octopus with pointed ears?

Spocktopus.

What about the electric octopus?

Shocktopus.

The night-time octopus?

Noctopus.

The octopus that likes Chinese cooking?

The Woktopus.

An octopus with a dress?

Frocktopus.

An octopus that gives the fish rides?

Octobus.

A worried octopus?
Octofuss.

A Scottish octopus?
Jocktopus.

An octopus with lots of keys?
Locktopus.

An octopus that tells the time?
Ticktocktopus.

An octopus that wakes you up in the morning?
Alarmclocktopus.

An octopus that cleans floors?
Moptopus.

An octopus shaped like a brick?
Blocktopus.

An octopus made from stone?
Rocktopus.

A law enforcement octopus?
Coptopus.

An octopus that eats too many Mars Bars?
Choctopus.

An octopus that eats too many Rice Krispies?
Snapcrackleandpoptopus.

An octopus with woollen feet warmers?
Socktopus.

The same octopus, who doesn't wash?
Smellysocktopus.

An octopus that always does its homework?
Swottopus.

An octopus with one leg?
Hoptopus.

An octopus that likes dancing?
Boptopus.

The Paul Daniels octopus?
You'regoingtolikethisnotalottopus.

The octopus taken in by another octopus family?
Adoptopus.

The octopus whose parents were a crocodile and a hippo?

Hippocroctopus.

The octopus that cannot dive?

Bellyfloptopus.

The octopus that you can only see when you join up
numbered points with a pencil?

Dot-to-dot-topus.

An octopus that flies upside down using its tentacles as rotary blades?
Helicoptopus.

A dinosaur octopus?

Triceratoptopus.

An octopus into martial arts?

Karatechoptopus.

An octopus with no legs and no body?

Ed.

Enough! I can't take any more
Jokes about the octopus
So make up your own puns
It's time for me to stoptopus.

Paul Cookson and 8MR, NK School, North Hykeham.